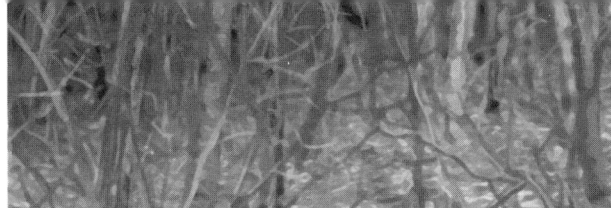

Cold Tom

Contents

A Letter from Sally Prue	3
Picture This!	4–5
What Does Your Environment Say About You?	6–7
Joe – Scientist in the Making or Cruel Bully?	8–9
Do You Believe It?	10–11
Urban Sprawl!	12–13
Cover Story	14–15
Pathways… to Another Good Read	16

OXFORD
UNIVERSITY PRESS

Great Clarendon Street, Oxford OX2 6DP

Oxford University Press is a department of the University of Oxford.
It furthers the University's objective of excellence in research,
scholarship, and education by publishing worldwide in

Oxford New York

Auckland Cape Town Dar es Salaam Hong Kong Karachi
Kuala Lumpur Madrid Melbourne Mexico City Nairobi
New Delhi Shanghai Taipei Toronto

With offices in

Argentina Austria Brazil Chile Czech Republic France Greece
Guatemala Hungary Italy Japan South Korea Poland Portugal
Singapore Switzerland Thailand Turkey Ukraine Vietnam

Oxford is a registered trade mark of Oxford University Press
in the UK and in certain other countries

Text © Julie Moxon 2007

The moral rights of the author have been asserted

Database right Oxford University Press (maker)

First published 2007

All rights reserved. No part of this publication may be reproduced,
stored in a retrieval system, or transmitted in any form or by any
means, without the prior permission in writing of Oxford
University
Press, or as expressly permitted by law, or under terms agreed with
the appropriate reprographics rights organization. Enquiries
concerning reproduction outside the scope of the above should be
sent
to the Rights Department, Oxford University Press, at the address
above.

You must not circulate this book in any other binding or cover and
you must impose this same condition on any acquirer.

British Library Cataloguing in Publication Data

Data available

ISBN 978 019 832686 1

10 9 8 7 6 5 4 3 2 1

Printed by Printplus, China.

Acknowledgements

The Publisher would like to thank the following for permission to reproduce photographs:

P3: Sally Prue.

Illustrations are by Q2A India.

Cover artwork is by Daniel Leary/Illustration

We are grateful for permission to reprint the following copyright material in this guide:

Sally Prue: extracts from *Cold Tom* (OUP, 2001), reprinted by permission of Oxford University Press; letter reprinted by permission of the author.

We have tried to trace and contact all copyright holders before publication. If notified, the publisher will be pleased to rectify any errors or omissions at the earliest opportunity.

Key to icons:

 Pair or group activity

 A resources sheet from the Teacher's Pack supports this activity.

A Letter from Sally Prue

Hello!

How nice to be able to write to you like this – usually a book has to speak for itself! I hope you'll find it interesting to know how *Cold Tom* began.

I started thinking about the book that became *Cold Tom* when I came across a really annoying article in a magazine. It said that people don't like each other – that is, that they only do nice things in the hope of getting something back. I really *didn't* believe this, but, however much I thought about it, I found I couldn't prove it one way or the other. In the end I thought I'd try writing about a community where everybody hates each other, and explore the idea that way.

The first thing I realized was that this couldn't be a human community, because all the babies would get abandoned. I needed a creature that was stronger at birth. I tried again with aliens, but I couldn't get that to work, either.

And then one day, I was having a quiet walk in Ashridge Forest when something big exploded, right at my feet – and it was a faun. (They're often left hiding in the grass, because their mothers only need to feed them occasionally.) And that was when I started thinking about the creatures of the woods…

This was much more promising, until I hit the next big problem. If they all hated each other, then how could a story develop?

It was clear that I had to get my hero fairly quickly into the human world.

Well, there are quite a few stories about elves and humans. Fairport Convention's *Liege and Lief* contains an exciting sung version of the legend of *Tam Lin*; and then, looking up the words in 'The Oxford Book Of English Verse', I accidentally came upon a terrific and terrifying poem called *Loving Mad Tom*. And that was when the elves really began to take on a life of their own.

It was fascinating following Tom, and seeing our world through his eyes. I got to think a lot about people and the way we live together. But the most important thing in writing the book was always the story – what happens, and all the *whys* that bind the whats together. I hope you enjoy following Tom's journey.

All best wishes,

Sally Prue

Sally Prue

Picture This!

Through Tom's Eyes

Much of the narrative of *Cold Tom* is seen through Tom's eyes, giving the reader a fresh look at a familiar world. Look at the examples below and work out with your partner what Tom is describing.

- *She pushed him at one of the stuffed things. It was so stuffed he didn't hurt himself when he fell into it. (page 64)*

- *The house had a latrine pool-thing that swallowed everything up in a great slurp of rushing water. (page 74)*

- *…the floor was covered in metallic strips and tiny boxes on wheels. (page 105)*

- *[The room] contained a huge padded pouch-thing that you were supposed to sleep in… (page 69)*

- *There was a box in the corner of the room with a web of wire across the front. There was something alive in it. (page 105)*

- *…they could shoot bolts of lead that smashed holes right through your body. (page 10)*

- *Through Edie's door he could see the square white box upon which she scorched her food. (page 108)*

- *…a cage of red-hot bars pulsed scorching heat… (page 64)*

- *The demon began to inspect its wad of paper, very carefully, a sheet at a time… (page 18)*

- *A whole house full of meat. A demon in white was giving some to another demon… There were bits of sheep arranged on white boards. (page 13)*

What do Tom's perceptions tell the reader about him as a character, his opinions of demons and his way of life?

Cold Tom

Picture This!

 Describe these objects from Tom's point of view.

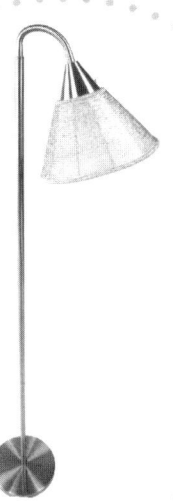
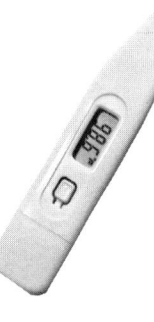

Quick Quiz

True or False?
1. The idea of a *house full of meat* (page 13) is disgusting to Tom.
2. Tom hates the idea of the vines that bind demons together (page 106).
3. The phrase *demon chariots* (page 9) suggests that the Tribe is still fairly primitive.
4. The phrase *scorched her food* (page 108) suggests that Tom thinks cooking food is a good idea.

Cold Tom

What Does Your Environment Say About You?

The Tribe's World

Viewpoint: Tom and the Tribe live outdoors. Their world is wild and cold, their characters seem cruel and emotionless.

Evidence:

A stag... steamed, new-dead (page 4)

scrubby blackthorn (page 1)

the chaffinch was flapping and fighting for its life (page 3)

tangle of thornbushes (page 2)

the saw-edges of the frosty grass (page 7)

The Demons' World

Viewpoint: The demons in the story are seen by Tom as being totally dependent on each other, connected by vines, yet living in opposition to nature.

Evidence:

plants were fenced and clipped (page 12)

rows of square clay houses (page 11)

the demons' road... was made of harsh grey stuff that had withered all the plants near it (page 10)

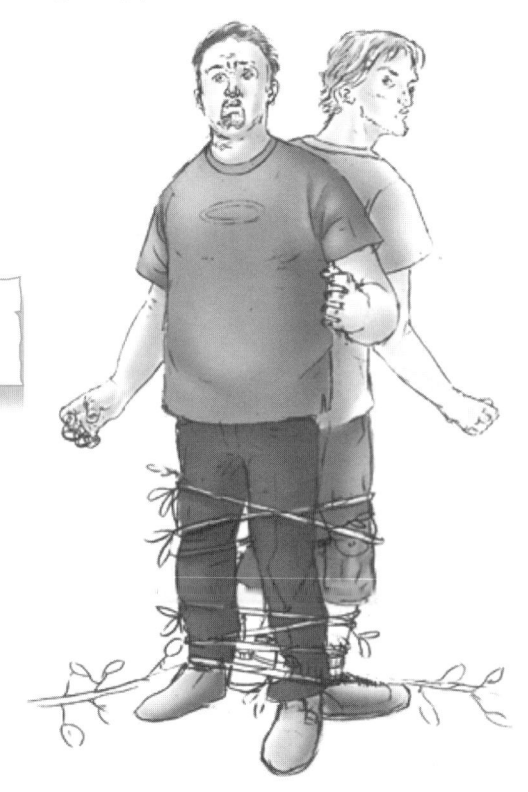

Do you agree with these views about the Tribe and the demons? As you read the novel, look out for evidence which supports or challenges these views.

What Does Your Environment Say About You?

Character Tracker

As you read *Cold Tom*, keep track of Joe's character and behaviour – which features are like those of the Tribe and which more like those of the demons?

> Joe had gone long and blue; and Tom realized, with a tingling shock, that now Joe could almost be one of the Tribe.
> (page 54)

> Joe walked quickly down towards the house after him and out of sight. It was as if he was pulled by a string that had suddenly thickened itself into a strong cable.
> (page 87)

Where Do You Belong? Tribe or Demon?

Dream holiday:
a Wild camping in the remote north
b Five-star luxury in a hot and sunny location

Favourite meal:
a Raw fish or rare steak
b Roast dinner and hot pudding

Perfect job:
a Anything as long as you are your own boss
b Anything that involves working with other people – teaching or nursing, maybe

Mostly **a** – You would be most likely to enjoy an outdoor lifestyle similar to the Tribe's. You are independent, resourceful and adventurous.

Mostly **b** – You are definitely best suited to the demons' style of life. You love company and being part of a group. You are dependable and caring.

Cold Tom

Joe – Scientist in the Making or Cruel Bully?

Lucky escape
A radio script

A young visitor from London narrowly escaped death when a shed he was playing in blew up. Our *Demon Radio* presenter caught up with Joe at his father's house earlier today.

Presenter: Joe, what exactly happened to cause the shed to blow up?

Joe: I was doing some research, but it was Tom who made the shed blow up. Not me.

Presenter: Tom? Is he a friend of yours?

Joe: No. He was… is… well, he isn't really human.

Presenter: Not human?

Joe: He makes himself invisible. That's what I was trying to find out. I wanted to know, scientifically, what happened to him.

Presenter: Can you explain what you did?

Joe: I took his temperature but the mercury disappeared and the thermometer was covered in frost. He didn't fade away, he just disappeared.

Presenter: Joe, you don't really believe people can become invisible? That only happens in stories like Harry Potter with his invisibility cloak.

Joe: I saw it. He must be as advanced as Einstein and Newton and Hawking.

Presenter: You seem very interested in science, Joe. Surely invisibility is a scientific impossibility?

Joe: No, it's not. I've read about it. Scientists are already looking into it. At Imperial College in London they've made designer atoms with specially chosen levels of energy in them. When light shines on these crystals it isn't absorbed and the material becomes transparent. It's a lot more complicated than that really, but that's the idea. When they can do it outside of the laboratory, they will be able to use it to look through rubble to find people who are trapped after an earthquake or something!

Presenter: That sounds really exciting, Joe. Would you like to do science for your GCSEs?

Joe: Yes, I'm going to be a scientist. All by myself. No family. Just facts.

What is Joe Really Like?

Joe seems to be a very unhappy, angry boy for most of the story. The other characters have their own opinions about him as you can see in the talking heads opposite.

 Discuss the feelings each character has about Joe.
- What do these feelings tell you about each of their relationships with him?
- What are your opinions about Joe?

Find some quotations to help you explain how you reached your conclusions.

Joe – Scientist in the Making or Cruel Bully?

"Joe thinks he's a scientist, but really he is a nasty bully. I hate him. I will never forgive him."

"It's been really difficult making Joe feel part of the family. He is so resentful that I live with Anna and not him. I don't know how to talk to him."

"Joe is like the Tribe. It wants to hurt, it enjoys killing. But he's not like the Tribe because he wants to enslave me."

"Joe is confused. It's only to be expected. It must be very difficult when you've come from a broken home."

"Joe's a good boy deep down. He is missing his mum, and his dad isn't used to him. They need to bond. He's probably missing the excitement of London as well."

Cold Tom

Do You Believe It?

Twentieth-century Fairies

Do you believe in fairies?
Do you believe in aliens and UFOs?
Some people believe they are the same thing and that the ancient stories were a way of explaining what people now say are alien abductions…

Similarities between aliens and elves and other 'little people':
- They kidnap people who then say they have 'lost' a period of time
- They sometimes use rods or wands to paralyse people before they abduct them
- They steal babies and sometimes leave a double or changeling in their place

Medieval Fairies

In medieval England, fairies and elves were thought to be dangerous, powerful and cruel. People believed they needed to perform rituals to protect themselves against them.

Fairies in Literature

Fairies might carry off children and adults to fairyland, which could be a frightening experience – and they could not return if they ate or drank anything there.

Quick Quiz
1. What evidence is there in the book that Tom and the elves may be connected with another planet?
2. Can you find an example of ritual protection in *Cold Tom*?

Do You Believe It?

Three fairypeople… How lovely their smiles are. How kind. And they are offering her refreshments — a ripe peach… a goblet of sweet cider… a handful of snow…
'No. No, thank you…' Don't give in, she tells herself. One sip… one bite and you'll never get home. You'll be here for evermore.

(Julie Hearn: The Merrybegot• – page 67)

In folklore, fairies are magical beings who often meddle in human affairs. Shakespeare used this idea for his creation of Puck in *A Midsummer Night's Dream*. Traditionally, Puck was a malicious and wicked fairy, but when Shakespeare used the character, he created a mischievous hobgoblin rather than a wicked one.

Nell, the main character, goes into fairyland to deliver a fairy baby. Her Granny gives her strict instructions about what to avoid in order to safely return to her own world.
*recommended read!

Puck: And sometime lurk I in a gossip's bowl
In very likeness of a roasted crab,
And, when she drinks, against her lips I bob,
And on her withered dewlap pour the ale.
The wisest aunt, telling the saddest tale,
Sometime for three-foot stool mistaketh me;
Then slip I from her bum, down topple she,

(Shakespeare: A Midsummer Night's Dream – Act 2, Scene 1)

Danish Fairies

When fog moves among the alder trees, it looks as if shapes are moving between them. In Denmark, people believed that these shapes were elves, dangerous creatures that put spells on people that could kill them!

It was said that if you saw an elven girl from the front she would be very beautiful, but from behind she would look like an alder trunk and have a hole in her back. Beautiful from the front, but empty and hollow from behind…

How would you describe the elves from Cold Tom? Kind or wicked?

Think of three adjectives to describe them. Find some examples of their behaviour to support your choice of adjectives.

As you read *Cold Tom*, think about whether the story has been influenced by some of these ideas about fairies.

Quick Quiz Answers

1. Tom calls on the stars when he needs to disappear.
2. Edie places alder branches across doors and windows to keep the Tribe out.

Urban Sprawl!

The Tribe are dwindling in number as their habitat is taken away by the demons' ever-increasing roads and houses.

Look around you. What do you see? Are you surrounded by woodland, fields and common land? Or is every square centimetre of green disappearing under concrete and houses?

Common Land – Who Does It Belong To?

1 Over 1,000 years ago, when Britain was mostly wooded, the great forests and rivers were open to everyone.

2 After the Norman Conquest, the manorial system was introduced and the land divided among the Lords of the Manor. People could no longer use the land and rivers as they wished.

3 Any land which wasn't required for agriculture, could be used by villagers to graze their animals or collect wood and turf for cooking and heating. This was known as common land, even though it was owned by landowners.

4 Commons still exist today, although not many people graze their animals on them or collect firewood! They are an important nature conservation asset and are often Sites of Special Scientific interest. People campaign strongly whenever there is the threat of losing more of our green land.

Urban Sprawl!

> **LOCAL COMMON IN DANGER OF DEVELOPMENT**
>
> It was a belief long held by the Tribe that demons would never build on the common – but they were getting closer all the time.
> (page 23)

Imagine planning permission is being sought to build a housing estate on the common. The Tribe is in danger of losing its home. Where would each of the characters stand on the issue? Who would be in favour? Who would be against and who might sit on the fence?

You could hold a public meeting for the characters to debate the proposal. You will need to search the novel to find evidence to support each point of view.

There are demon outposts* all around the woods and scrubby heaths of the common now. This has been our home for centuries!
(*demon outposts, page 2)

The demons are increasing. Every year there are more. And they are no longer afraid. They are forgetting the tales that have kept them in fear for so long.
(page 20)

Cold Tom

Cover Story

Front cover: Scholastic Trade edition of *Cold Tom*

Author's comments

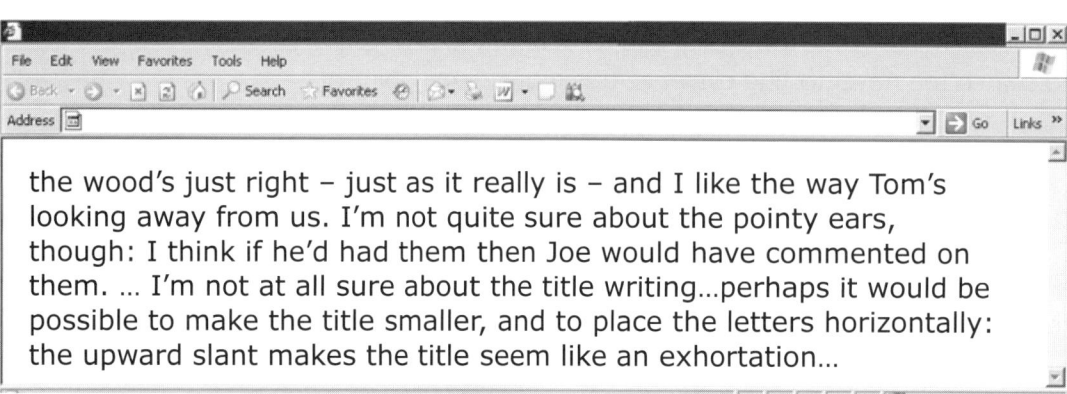

the wood's just right – just as it really is – and I like the way Tom's looking away from us. I'm not quite sure about the pointy ears, though: I think if he'd had them then Joe would have commented on them. ... I'm not at all sure about the title writing...perhaps it would be possible to make the title smaller, and to place the letters horizontally: the upward slant makes the title seem like an exhortation...

Front cover: Oxford University Press Trade edition of *Cold Tom*.

Cover Story

Front cover: Oxford University Press Rollercoasters edition of *Cold Tom*.

Imagine you have been sent these covers for your comments before a final decision is made. What do you think of them?

Remember that the book is aimed at an audience of young adults of about the same age as you. How relevant are the covers to the story of *Cold Tom*?

- What do you like about each cover?
- Does it give enough clues about the theme or mood of the book?
- What doesn't work? Explain why.
- How could the covers be improved? Justify your suggestions, with details from *Cold Tom*.

Pathways… to Another Good Read

Online texts
The Legend of Tam Lin – put the title into a search engine and take your pick!

Works by the same author
Goldkeeper
ISBN 0-19-271950-5
Sebastian is a boy who revels in mischief, so it is a shock to everyone when he is apprenticed to the High Priest at The Temple of Ora. Does he get down to his studies, or is life in the temple changed beyond recognition?

James and the Alien Experiment
ISBN 0-7136-7457-1
In Cold Tom, Joe experiments on Tom the changeling, but in this book it is earthling James who is experimented on by his kidnappers!

Thematically linked texts
The Merrybegot by Julie Hearn
ISBN 0-19-279157-5
Julie Hearn tells the story of a young girl who is different. Like Tom, she inhabits two worlds; she too has links with the fairy world, but in this world, she lives in danger, accused of being a witch! (An extract from this book can be found on page 11 of this Reading Guide.)

Skellig by David Almond
ISBN 0-3409-0554-9
A stranger is found in a crumbling garage – he doesn't hold conversations in the usual way and he has wings! Michael and Mina befriend him and bring him food. This is the start of a new life for them all.

And if you enjoy folklore try these: *Sir Gawain and the Green Knight*; *The Hobbit* by J R R Tolkien; The *Artemis Fowl* series by Eoin Colfer; The *Harry Potter* series by J K Rowling; *The Chronicles of Narnia* by C.S. Lewis.

Family Life:
The Suitcase Kid by Jacqueline Wilson
ISBN 0-4408-6311-2
In *Cold Tom*, Joe is finding life hard now that his Dad has remarried. Here is another story which looks at life when parents have divorced and the children have to learn to live with new family members.

A Visit to the Theatre
See how Shakespeare portrays fairies in two of his plays: *A Midsummer Night's Dream* and *The Tempest*.

Happy reading!